I didn't know that wolves howl at the Moon

© Aladdin Books Ltd 2000
Produced by
Aladdin Books Ltd
28 Percy Street
London W1P 0LD

ISBN 0-7496-3425-1
First published in Great Britain in 2000 by
Aladdin Books/Watts Books
96 Leonard Street
London EC2A 4XD

Concept, editorial and design by

David West Children's Books

Designer: Jennifer Skelly
Illustrators: Mike Atkinson, Jo Moore

Printed in Belgium

I didn't know that

wolves howl at the Moon

Cecilia Fitzsimons

Aladdin / Watts
London • Sydney

I didn't know that

Introduction

Did *you* know that at night vampire bats hunt for blood? ... that fennec foxes sleep all day under the sand? ... that owls can hunt through the night without making a sound?

Discover for yourself amazing facts about all sorts of creatures of the night – who they are, how they hunt, what they eat and more.

Look out for this symbol which means there is a fun project for you to try.

Is it true or is it false? Watch for this symbol and try to answer the question before reading on for the answer.

Don't forget to check the borders for extra amazing facts.

I didn't know that

some animals only come out at night. Foxes and racoons are *nocturnal* - they come out to hunt at night. Other animals like cats also come out at night.

At night some worms crawl out from their burrows. They grab a fallen leaf and pull it underground.

SEARCH & FIND
Can you find six mice?
FIND & SEARCH

Racoon

Fox

Rat

Badger

Hedgehog

6

In prehistoric times, *mammals* only existed as tiny shrew-like animals, hunted by small dinosaurs. Like shrews, they may have been nocturnal – active by night while the dinosaurs rested. After the dinosaurs died out, mammals and birds became the most successful animals.

Wild hamsters and gerbils live in burrows underground. At night they come out and run around. You may know this, if you have a pet hamster because they sometimes keep their owners awake by running on their exercise wheel at night!

Cat

Your eyes can adjust to help you see in the dark. Look at your eyes in a mirror. Face a bright window. Move away and turn into a darkened room. See how your *pupil* changes size.

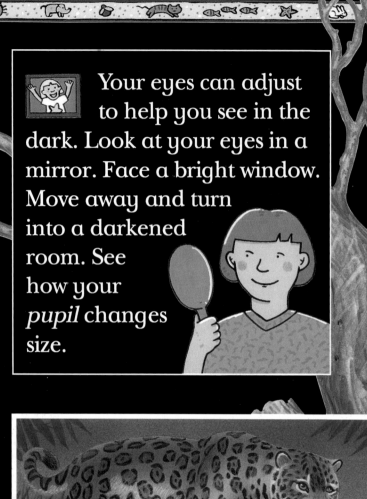

Jaguars live in the rainforests of South America. Here they hunt for many types of animal, such as peccary (a wild pig), deer, caiman (a type of crocodile), monkeys and fish.

Most big cats hunt at night. Each tiger hunts alone. *Camouflaged* by its stripes, the tiger hides in the long grass. When a pig, deer or buffalo wanders past, the tiger rushes out and attacks.

I didn't know that

leopards hunt at night.

They live throughout much of Africa and Asia, and prey upon animals of all shapes and sizes – from insects to antelope. Larger prey are dragged up into a tree and will feed a leopard for several days.

True or false?

Cats' eyes glow in the dark.

Answer: **False**

Cats' pupils open wide at night. As light is reflected from the back of the eyes, they seem to glow.

Cats use their whiskers to sense air movement and their prey in the dark.

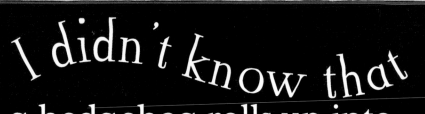

I didn't know that

a hedgehog rolls up into a spiky ball. At night if danger threatens it tucks its legs, head and soft belly safely inside, protected by a mass of sharp spines. It sleeps like this during the day.

True or false?

Opossums play dead.

Answer: **True**

If attacked the Virginia opossum rolls over on its back, shuts its eyes and flops out its tongue. It pretends to be dead, which we call 'playing possum'.

Hedgehog

Pangolins are covered from head to tail with an armour of tough, sharp-edged scales. When frightened, these slow-moving insect-eaters simply curl up tight until the danger has passed.

All skunks are patterned with bold black and white stripes. This is a warning to *predators* to 'stay away'. Skunks are active at night, they defend themselves by squirting a jet of the most dreadful smelling scent at their attacker.

Packs of spotted hyenas hunt and scavenge by night. They sound as if they are laughing, as they keep in touch with each other by making a wide variety of calls that include whoops, cackles, grunts and moans.

At dusk, before they sleep, troops of South American howler monkeys howl a loud chorus from the treetops. They are proclaiming their territory and can be heard up to five kilometres away.

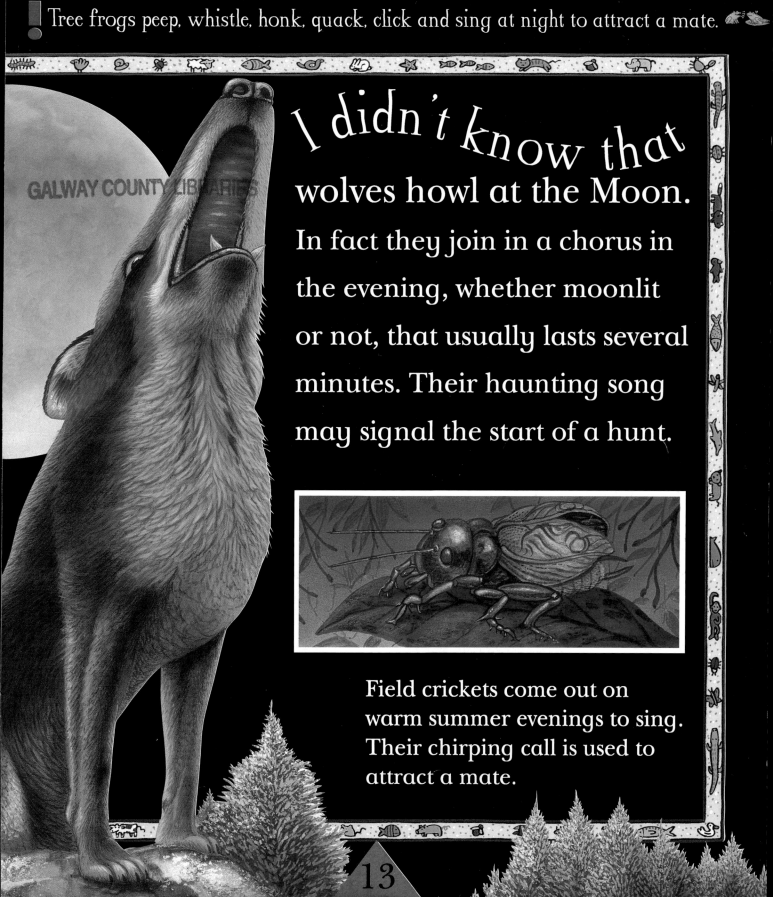

I didn't know that wolves howl at the Moon. In fact they join in a chorus in the evening, whether moonlit or not, that usually lasts several minutes. Their haunting song may signal the start of a hunt.

Field crickets come out on warm summer evenings to sing. Their chirping call is used to attract a mate.

13

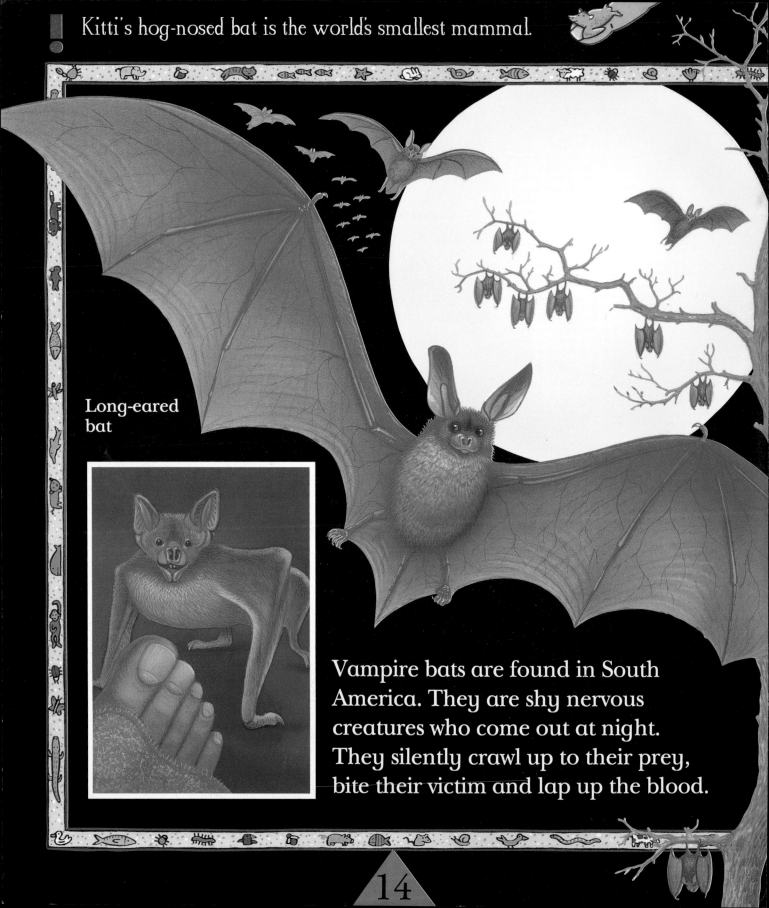

Long-eared
bat

Vampire bats are found in South
America. They are shy nervous
creatures who come out at night.
They silently crawl up to their prey,
bite their victim and lap up the blood.

I didn't know that

bats see with their ears. They use *echolocation* (*sonar*) to guide them through the night. The bats make *ultrasonic* clicking noises. They can detect the position of a moth by judging the speed of the echo.

The South American fishing bat swoops down and plucks a fish from the river below. It uses sonar to pinpoint ripples on the surface of the water.

 True or false?
All bats are blind.

Answer: **False**
Bats can see, but their sonar is more useful than sight when they fly at night.

SEARCH & FIND & FIND & SEARCH & Can you find eight upside-down bats?

 Some moths make ultrasonic clicking noises which confuse a bat's sonar.

True or false?

Owls swallow their prey whole.

Answer: **True**

Owls swallow all of their prey - the bits that can't be digested, such as bones, are *regurgitated* later.

One of the most *endangered* birds in the world is the kakapo, a large, flightless parrot from New Zealand. Kakapos are nocturnal. By burrowing underground during the day, they hide from daytime predators such as eagles.

Barn owl

The fruit-eating oilbird has big eyes to see in the dark. It also emits clicks and uses sonar when flying at night. Oilbirds nest in caves in South America.

I didn't know that owls fly silently through the night, swooping down on prey that never hears them coming. Their wing feathers have a comb-like fringe to soften any wind noise made during flight.

17

True or false?

Snakes taste the air.

Answer: **True**

A snake flicks its tongue in and out, collecting chemicals in the air. The tongue wipes them on the *Jacobson's organ* in the roof of the mouth and produces a sensation of smell.

Jacobson's organ

The egg-eating snake swallows whole eggs by dislocating its jaw. In its throat, a row of sharp bones slice open the shell. The snake regurgitates the shell after it has drained the yolk.

Pit viper

In the South American rainforest, the rainbow boa hunts at night for small birds or mammals. Like its relative the boa constrictor, the rainbow boa kills its prey by squeezing it – tight within its coils.

I didn't know that

rattlesnakes have heat detectors to find their prey. Deep pits on their face see an image of an animal's warm body like the picture from an infrared camera. This helps them to hunt at night.

Bolas spider

The bolas spider catches moths at night. It spins a line of silk with blobs of glue on the end. The spider swings the thread around and throws it at a passing moth – which is caught in the blob of glue.

The fastest moths are hawk moths. They can fly more than 50 km per hour. The skull-like pattern on the death's-head hawk moth's thorax gives this moth its grim name.

True or false?

Some moths dive to avoid bats.

Answer: **True**
Some moths nose dive straight at the ground to avoid a hungry bat, and hide there until it is safe.

The deathwatch beetle bangs its head on wood to attract its mate.

I didn't know that

moths are attracted to light bulbs. They become dazzled and confused by the bright lights, so they blunder around and fly towards them.

When it is dark, hang a white sheet from a washing line or over a rope between two trees. Shine a bright light on to it. Watch the moths settle on to the circle of light.

Tropical moon moth

GALWAY COUNTY LIBRARIES

As night falls tiny *planktonic* plants and animals float upwards to feed in the surface waters of the sea. Jellyfish follow them to feed. At daybreak they sink back down.

SEARCH & FIND
Can you find five fish?
FIND & SEARCH

Sand tiger shark

Jellyfish

Horseshoe crab

Swarms of horseshoe crabs *migrate* to their breeding beaches in America and Asia. For three nights, by the light of the full Moon, they mate and lay their eggs in the sand before returning to the sea.

Turtles patrol the open oceans but return to land to breed. At night, females drag themselves up the beach and dig a deep hole in the sand to lay their eggs.

Green turtle

I didn't know that coral comes out at night to feed. A coral reef is built by *colonies* of tiny sea animals called polyps. They open their tentacles to trap food and waft it into their mouth.

I didn't know that

some animals glow in the dark. They are able to use a special process called *bioluminescence* to generate cold light in their body.

Glow-worms and fireflies are types of beetle. The tip of their abdomen flashes a yellow or green light to attract a mate.

Glow-worm

Firefly

Flashlight fish

Many deep-sea animals have light-producing organs called *photophores*. Flashlight fish can turn their photophores on and off. Different types of flash help the fish to identify friend or foe, food or mate in the darkness around them.

Minute glowing organisms called noctiluca live in the plankton and produce light as the water moves. Swarms of them can make the sea glow and sparkle behind a boat.

 True or false?

It is not just animals that glow in the dark.

Answer: **True**

Luminous toadstools such as the Jack O' Lantern from America and the Australian ghost fungus grow and glow on forest floors.

True or false?
Catfish walk on land.

Answer: **True**
Some catfish crawl from drying ponds to find water. They use their pectoral fins as legs.

Snails and slugs are called gastropods because they move on their tummy. Gastropod means 'stomach-foot'.

Eels can travel across country from pond to river by crawling through wet grass. On land, they close their gills in much the same way as we 'hold our breath' when under water.

Slug

26

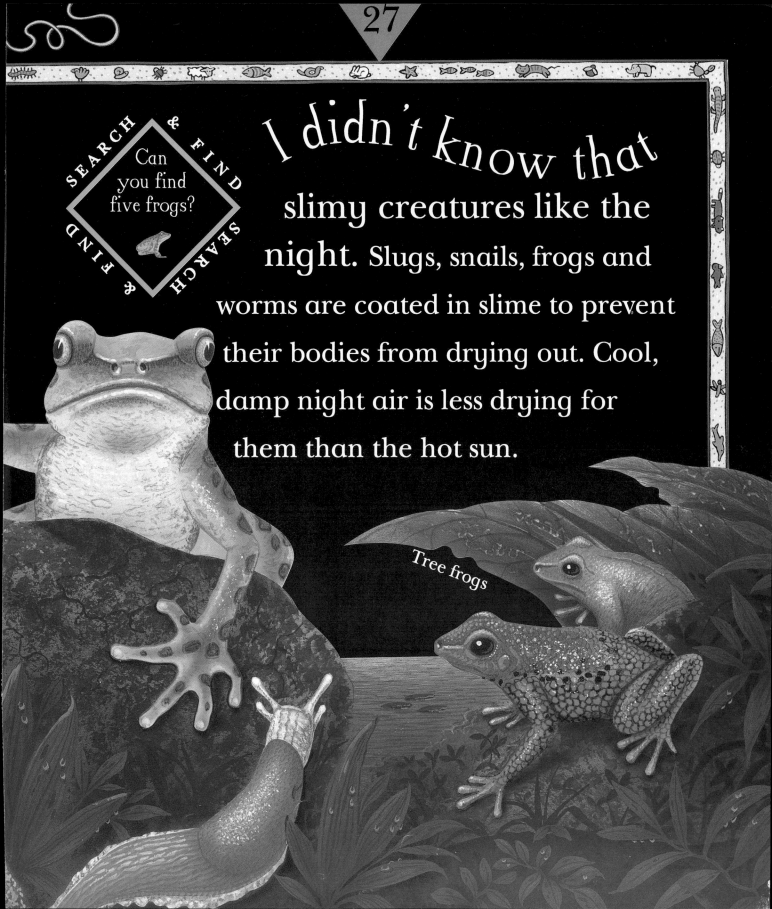

SEARCH & FIND & FIND & SEARCH

Can you find five frogs?

I didn't know that

slimy creatures like the night. Slugs, snails, frogs and worms are coated in slime to prevent their bodies from drying out. Cool, damp night air is less drying for them than the hot sun.

Tree frogs

I didn't know that

some animals sleep during the day. Most animals, like wild cats, that hunt at night will sleep during the day. Lions spend much of the day asleep, conserving their energy before they start to hunt again.

Bats fall into a deep sleep every day. To avoid predators, they roost together in a hollow tree or cave or under a roof.

Many geckos are active at night. They hide in cracks in walls, rocks and bark during the day.

 True or false?
Kangaroos sleep in trees.

Answer: **True**
Tree kangaroos live in the rainforests of Northern Australia and New Guinea. They sleep all day, high on a branch, and wake up at night to feed.

Tiny fennec foxes rest in a cool den, burrowed deep into the desert sand. At night, their huge ears pick up the slightest rustle of lizards and other small prey.

 Dwarf puff adders bury themselves in the sand to avoid the Sun's heat.

Glossary

Bioluminescence
Light produced by some animals, made by chemical reactions inside their body.

Camouflage
The colours and markings on an animal which help it to blend in with its surroundings and make it difficult to see.

Colony
A group of animals that live so closely to one another that they share the same lifestyle and food. Individual members of a colony may be unable to exist alone and their bodies may be joined together.

Echolocation
Using sound to 'see' in total darkness by sending out short clicking noises. A sound picture is created by comparing the speed of the echo that returns.

Endangered
Animals and plants that are so rare that they will become extinct if they are not protected.

Jacobson's organ
Pits in the roof of a snake's mouth. Used to smell food.

Mammal
An animal, such as a shrew, which gives birth to live young that it feeds on milk.

Migrate
To travel a long distance from one place to another, often to breed.

Nocturnal
Being active at night.

Photophore
Part of an animal's body that is used to produce light.

Plankton
Tiny animals and plants that live by floating in the sea or fresh water.

Predator
An animal which catches and eats other animals.

Pupil
The central black part of the eye. It is a hole by which light passes into the eye.

Regurgitate
To eat something, swallow it, then bring it back up into the mouth. The item may then be spat out or swallowed again.

Sonar
Another name for echo-location, especially if used under water.

Ultrasonic
Very high-pitched, squeaking sounds. Often too high for the human ear to hear.

Index